My Favorite Machine
FIRE TRUCKS

Victoria Marcos

xist Publishing

Published in the United States by Xist Publishing
www.xistpublishing.com
PO Box 61593 Irvine, CA 92602

First Edition
Hardcover ISBN: 9781532410710
Paperback ISBN: 9781532405532
eISBN: 9781532405549

Table of Contents

My favorite machines are fire trucks. Would you like to learn about them?

Fire trucks are big trucks that carry firefighters and special tools.

They are used to fight fires and help in emergencies.

MAX. 110 KG.

7.5 BAR

They carry tools like ladders, hoses, helmets, and first aid kits.

Do You Remember?

What do fire trucks do?

Check and see if you're right at
the end of this book!

Fire trucks use very loud sirens and flashing lights to warn people that a fire truck is on its way.

When a fire truck pulls up to a fire, the firefighters connect a very long hose to the fire hydrant.

They turn on the water and spray the fire until it goes out.

Do You Remember?

What do fire trucks carry?

Check and see if you're right at
the end of this book!

In some areas, there are no fire hydrants. The fire truck needs to bring its own water.

Sometimes a fire is high up where the fire fighters can't reach from the ground. They need to use a very tall ladder.

There are many different types of fire trucks: conventional, aerial, wildland, robot, and many more. This is a robot fire truck.

Do You Remember?

What does a fire hydrant supply to a fire truck?

Check and see if you're right at
the end of this book!

My favorite thing about fire trucks is that they can help in many ways. There is a fire truck for every emergency.

What is your favorite thing about fire trucks?

Glossary

Aerial fire truck: Fire truck with a tall ladder attached used to reach very high places

Conventional fire truck: Most common fire truck

Emergency: A serious and dangerous situation that needs attention right away

Fire hydrant: Something that fire fighters connect their hoses to get water

Wildland fire truck: Fire truck used in the forest

Did You Remember?

Answers:
Question #1:
Fight Fires and help in emergencies
Question #2:
Ladders, hoses, helmets and first aid kits
Question #3:
Water